BETTER THAN BLESSED ✍

BETTER THAN BLESSED

Drawn from the Beatitudes

DONALD L. ANDERSON, PH.D.

Tyndale House
Publishers, Inc.
Wheaton, Illinois

Library of Congress Catalog Card
Number 80-52238
ISBN 0-8423-0144-5, paper
Copyright © 1981 by Donald L.
Anderson
All rights reserved.

First printing, January 1981
Printed in the United States of America.

To Jeanne . . .
who understands.

CONTENTS

PREFACE

I live in two worlds. As a minister, I live in a world of faith, with people of faith. As a psychologist, I live in a world where science, or at least the scientific method, is god. And I am appalled at the chasm of misunderstanding and distrust that exists between these two worlds. The responsibility for the creation and maintenance of the chasm rests on both sides—religion and psychology—but the issues that divide them are varied and their history is long and stormy.

Strange as it may seem, psychology emerged as a definable science only one hundred years ago. It was in 1879 in Leipzig, Germany, that the first psychological laboratory was established by Wilhelm Wundt. His search for the "building blocks of the mind" was a long way from what most of us regard as legitimate psychology. It remained for the creative mind and prolific pen of Sigmund Freud, more than twenty years later, to produce the kind of inquiry and theorizing that most people associate with real psychology. So you see, psychology is really an infant in the family of science.

The emergence of psychology as a science was delayed by the antagonistic attitude of organized religion. For several dark centuries in Europe, the established church claimed the study of the soul of man as its exclusive, divinely established right. Not only did it make and enforce this claim, but churchmen defined "soul" in such a way as to make any study of man outside their defined limits an impossibility. In an attempt to break free from this restraint, some strange theories were presented. One can sympathize with a religious man like Descartes, who tried to break out of the cage with his theory of interactionism. When the *Zeitgeist* (spirit of the age) did change, and psychology's day dawned, it is understandable that its champions were angry with the church. In fact, the new science was born in conflict with organized religion.

The battle between religion and psychology is based on more, however, than the bad blood of conflicts centuries old. There are current and substantive issues that divide us. One of these divisive issues is particularly grating to me. It's the idea proposed by many behavioral scientists that faith is always a compromise with mental health. These accusers of the faith and the faithful have been unscientifically willing to generalize about all of Christendom from their experiences with a few disturbed disciples. Of course, not all Christians are mentally healthy—as are not all engineers,

Chinese, atheists, or psychologists. I am committed, though, to the thesis that proper understanding and practicing of the Christian faith enhances, not diminishes, one's mental health. If a person understands what Jesus is saying in the Gospels and tries to follow him and his teachings, he can achieve a degree of mental health and happiness unavailable to those without faith.

I hope this book supports this idea, which is its main purpose.

ONE
*Better
Than
Blessed*

ঽ

I was well into my middle years before I really began to appreciate the meaning and richness of those statements of introduction to the Sermon on the Mount that we call the beatitudes.

I met the beatitudes early in my life and memorized them long before they had any meaning for me. My father was a Baptist minister, and the church he pastored used to have at least one stem-winding revival every year. Usually, this involved importing evangelistic talent. These outside experts always organized the children into what was called the Sunshine Band, or the Booster Club. We children would learn gospel choruses, memorize Scripture, and enroll our school friends in this after-school program. Then on a well-publicized night, we would perform in the evening service to demonstrate what we had learned in those after-school sessions. This was a sure way to have a lot of "prospects" in the service. All the Sunshine Band would be there—and so would their parents.

It was in a Sunshine Band that I first memorized the beatitudes. You see, you got points for attendance, bringing new members, and learning portions of the Bible. The truth is, I think I must have earned points for the beatitudes in several different revivals. The outside talent, being new each year, had no way of knowing I had "memorized" the beatitudes for several previous years.

The re-memorization of the same Scripture doesn't seem quite right as I look back on it, but

I really wanted the unusual prizes that were offered for large point totals. I received some great ones, too—like a very small telescope you could hold up to the light and read most of the Ten Commandments. Then, there was the world's smallest Gospel of John and a little cross that glowed in the dark to remind you to say your prayers. (It frightened me more nights than it reminded me.)

I have a vivid memory of one of those frightening experiences. We were living in the Midwest then—in central Illinois to be exact—and the summer thunderstorms that sweep through that area are legendary. As a boy, I remember hearing the thunder in the distance and waiting anxiously for the storm to move closer. I never wanted to admit to anyone—even myself—that I was afraid when the thunder was loud and the lightning flashed in my room—but I was. When a storm came, I would curl up in a little ball in my bed and wait for it to be over. I liked the coolness and the smells that followed the storms, but all that noise and light were a bit much for me.

It was during one of those pyrotechnic displays that it happened. With the roll of the threatening thunder in the distance, I got ready to ride out the storm—and the fear. When I raised up to pull the covers over my head, I saw it. Something was glowing eerily on the other side of the room. The storm was frightening enough, but now there was an added ingredient—that mysterious and scary light in the darkness.

Minutes passed—minutes crowded with genuine and paralyzing fear (and some prayers)—before it dawned on me that it was my prize that was scaring me. That precious glow-in-the-dark cross for which I had "memorized" the beatitudes was doing its thing. At that moment it was more than a reminder to pray. It was a ghost, an unexplained and frightening presence to an already apprehensive boy. It took several tense minutes for me to remember that light in the night was really a cross mounted on cardboard that had gone unnoticed until the storm came.

Such was the nature of some of my first experiences with the beatitudes. I met them early and often in my life, and they were stowed away quite securely in my memory. My young friends and I used to refer to them as "the blesseds" and most of us could rattle them off. But they had no meaning—at least for me. To be "blessed" seemed like something little old ladies might long for, but there was no romance in "blessedness" for a boy.

So I was pleased when new translations of the New Testament came, and "blessed" was translated "happy." I may not have been bucking for blessedness, but I had always wanted to be happy. Still, it all failed to compute for me. "Happy are those who mourn" just didn't make a lot of sense, and I failed to understand how spiritual poverty could be thrilling. As an adult, I still treated the beatitudes rather lightly. The words were beautiful—and the ideas not very relevant.

Then I reached the preacher era of my life, and every preacher has to have a series of sermons on the beatitudes. They sound so impressive, and almost everyone knows them. And what pastor doesn't need eight ideas for sermons?

So I had my sermon series, too. I labored mightily, but I didn't come forth with a lot to say. It seemed to me that I was trying to explain paradoxes with paradoxes. The sermons may have sounded all right, properly serious and spiritual, but I knew that they lacked strong, relevant content. I was disappointed in myself and in my preaching. Even my attempts to explain them had further alienated me from the beatitudes.

One day, impressed with my new Ph.D. and a license to practice psychology, I decided I would attempt to read the New Testament from the point of view of a behavioral scientist. I had read it devotionally, and I had read it in search of sermon material. But this was to be a new experience for me. When I got to the fifth chapter of Matthew, I again had what had become a conditioned "turn off" to the beatitudes—they were beautiful, but esoteric and lacking in meaning for a modern man. Then an idea struck me. Maybe these were statements about emotional health. Could they be read as, *"Healthy* are those who know they are spiritually poor. . . . *Healthy* are those who mourn," and if read that way, would they have meaning for me?

So I changed that bothersome word "happy," and—Eureka!—the stately old beatitudes came to life for me. They made sense. Jesus was talking about Christian life style. This is what the Sermon on the Mount is all about! It was clear, tough instruction in how Jesus' followers were to relate to God, to themselves, to those who shared their faith, and to those who didn't. And the beatitudes can be viewed as the essence of what is stated in chapters five, six, and seven of the Gospel of Matthew—the body of that "sermon." Jesus was teaching his disciples how to live as healthy people in a very sick world. This was preventive medicine.

Much of what Jesus taught in eight terse statements was "discovered" by professionals in the twentieth century as part of the mental health movement. When the emerging science of psychology became associated with the treatment of mental illness through the work and writing of Sigmund Freud near the turn of the century, the discipline focused on mental illness and cure. It took more than a generation for the behavioral scientists to invest much energy in asking how they could prevent persons from becoming emotionally ill. Only with the emergence of this new concern could the mental health movement that began in the thirties really come into its own. Then psychologists were able to begin to work toward helping people develop a constructive philosophy about life (and death), strong supportive relationships, and attitudes about themselves that would keep them out of the psychotherapist's office. Jesus was 1900 years ahead of his time when he laid down the principles for healthy living found in the beatitudes. He was a first-century mental health crusader.

This should not be startling to people of faith. The Psalmist said, "He knows our frame. . . ." A part of the purpose of the Incarnation was for God to show us and tell us how to live as his healthy children in this world. He doesn't want miserable, confused, and emotionally disturbed children; so he had to give us some insights into how to live with ourselves and with others. And give them he did.

I am amazed at how well the beatitudes correlate with the secular literature on healthy behavior. It serves to remind me that our pseudosophistication can sometimes lead us away from the real source of truth. It has become more popular in many circles to quote Freud than Jesus. To allude to a book on personality theory seems more respectable than to quote from the Bible. Indeed, for some, Eric Berne, with his principles of Transactional Analysis, is the master teacher.

It is not, of course, an either/or proposition. One needs all he can learn from the world of science to carry back to the Scriptures. To function at the highest level a person must be a constant student of both the "secular" and the "sacred." Both Scripture and secular knowledge take on new and fresh meanings when they interact in the mind of a searching, growing person.

Take, for instance, the study of human life. Physiologists and physicians are constantly uncovering new information about the human body. It is a finely tuned machine. Its self-healing powers are remarkable, and it withstands the insults of modern life with incredible success. Any student of human life is awed by the capacities of our bodies.

Those, however, who are equipped to place man at the loftiest height are those who see the human being not as the representative of the highest order of evolution but as the creation—however accomplished—of a loving and purposeful God. One stands, then, not just awed by the human machine—but both by it and by the genius of its Designer. Reverence for life reaches new heights when that life is viewed as being here not by chance, but by divine plan. The person in whom scientific knowledge and faith converge experiences consummate awe in the presence of human life. The scientist without faith may understand the "hows" of life, but the scientist with faith has come to grips with the "hows" *and* the "whys."

Let's go back to the world of behavioral science for a minute. What do the students of human behavior say about mental health? In other words, how can a mentally healthy person be described?

I have found such definitions hard to uncover. Freud said that the healthy person is "able to work and to love." In a book published in 1974, S. Jourard defined the healthy personality in this way: "Healthy personality is a way for a person to act, guided by intelligence and respect for life, so that his needs are satisfied and he will grow in awareness, competence and the capacity for love."

After surveying the literature, I am convinced that behavioral scientists ascribe at least seven qualities to healthy people.

1. THEY AGREE WITH THE MAJORITY ABOUT REALITY.

The healthy are oriented to time and place. They know who they are, where they are, and when it all is happening. The healthy do not suffer from delusions or hallucinations.

2. THEY DEAL ADEQUATELY WITH THE PAST.

These healthy people are not carrying a load of guilt or hostility based on past events. They live in the present and deal with current issues.

3. THEY ARE PRODUCTIVE.

As Freud said, they are able to work. They are not so consumed by their inner conflicts that they have no strength left for work. For the healthiest, work is an end in itself, and is itself rewarding to them.

4. THEY ARE ABLE TO GIVE AND RECEIVE LOVE.

If to love is to be vulnerable, they run the risk of vulnerability. It is no disgrace to them to feel deeply for another. To be loved, for the healthy person, is not to feel limited and burdened.

5. THEY ACCEPT RESPONSIBILITY.

The responsible, healthy person is able to shoulder a task—an assignment—and to carry it out to completion. These people, also, are willing to assume responsibility for their own behavior. They will claim proper credit for their successes and assume personal responsibility for their failures. They will not play the "Ah, shucks, it was nothing" or "Whom can I blame when I am miserable or when I fail" kind of game.

6. THEY ACCEPT CHANGE.

The inevitable changes in the world, the family, and in themselves (brought about by aging) are not overly disturbing to them. They adapt to a changing society, a changing family, and an aging body without feeling out of place or useless.

7. THEY HAVE DEVELOPED A PHILOSOPHY OR FAITH WITH REGARD TO THEIR OWN DEATH.

They are not so afraid of dying that they cannot enjoy living. They view death as a natural and inevitable event in their existence.

Large books have been written attempting to describe mentally healthy persons. Frankly, I still don't know exactly how the healthiest among us look, feel, and act. I can tell you this, though. When you find a person who is emotionally healthy, that person will be as well described by the eight statements of Jesus called the beatitudes as by any compilation of attributes made by a contemporary scientist. Such a person may not totally possess all these qualities—but he will be on the way.

[Healthy] are those who know they are spiritually poor; the Kingdom of heaven belongs to them!
[Healthy] are those who mourn; God will comfort them!
[Healthy] are the meek; they will receive what God has promised!
[Healthy] are those whose greatest desire is to

do what God requires; God will satisfy them fully!

[Healthy] are those who are merciful to others; God will be merciful to them!

[Healthy] are the pure in heart; they will see God!

[Healthy] are those who work for peace among men; God will call them his sons!

[Healthy] are those who are persecuted because they do what God requires; the Kingdom of heaven belongs to them!

(Matt. 5:3-10, *Good News For Modern Man*)

TWO
The Struggling Christian

*"Happy are those
who know they are   ஐ
spiritually poor . . ."*

Jim was a very get-right-to-the-point kind of person. In response to my suggestion that he assume a position of leadership in the church, he responded without hesitation, "I can't do that. There are too many things still wrong in my life. A position like that is for persons who are better than I!"

My response to this refusal was—and still would be—to tell my friend that the church does not need leaders who have it made. The church needs leaders who are honest strugglers. The fact is that true Christianity has suffered more at the hands of the falsely pious than it ever has at the hands of the admittedly struggling sinful.

You will be pleased to know that Jim thought and prayed for awhile, then changed his mind. He accepted the position and has done a superb job. He still will tell you that he's no saint—just a struggler who wants to be better than he is.

It is this very kind of person that the first beatitude is addressing. The *Good News for Modern Man* version states it this way: "Happy are those who know they are spiritually poor." My paraphrase would read, "Healthy are those who know they do not have it made."

For a relatively long time, those who study human behavior have talked about the psychological mechanisms we all employ in the defense of our egos. While every person may use these defense mechanisms—denial, projection, reaction formation, etc.—we do know that the healthiest persons among us use them less frequently and less intensely than those who are emotionally disturbed. In the first beatitude,

Jesus is talking about the Christian's need to employ *denial* as an ego defense.

We have all observed persons using denial. There is the man who is very ill, but denies the gravity of his illness. Or, perhaps, the woman who probably is going to die as the result of a disease, but talks about her plans for the distant future. For these persons, reality is just too grim. They feel at a subconscious level that facing up to it is more than they can bear; so they defend themselves with the use of denial. What is obvious to others, they refuse to admit as reality; and no argument can persuade them that they have an unreal view of their world.

Transfer this inability to face reality into the arena of the Christian life, and you can trace the lineage of the denier from Jesus' day to ours. All the spiritual progeny of the scribes and Pharisees have not died out. As in a vignette Jesus told, the spiritually poor are still at prayer saying, "God be merciful to me, a sinner"—and the users of denial are praying (and feeling honest in doing so), "I thank you that I am better than others."

The well-meaning disciple gets pushed into using denial in at least two ways. First, he wants to live **up to** the demands the Scriptures make of him. There is the desire to be "holy" as God is "holy." He may interpret the injunction to be "perfect" to mean "sinless" instead of its proper meaning—"mature." The very drive toward Christlikeness that is the result of his faith pushes him toward the trap. It is painful to know that you are not holy—that you are far

28

from "perfect." So denial is employed, and the discomfort is reduced. It does not usually produce the exaggerated response of claiming perfection, but it does allow the person to compare himself with others and look and feel good in the process. It allows a stance of spiritual superiority from which one can view other Christians with pity and condescension. His message to the rest of us is now a godlike one. "Be ye holy as *I* am holy."

The other way we get caught in the denial trap is through our interpersonal aspirations. Somewhere in every Christian is the desire to be a winner in the church. We want to be well thought of by those we respect—and we would like to have our spiritual accomplishments rewarded with official positions. The route of the hypocrite is objectionable; so we elect to go with denial. This is not a conscious decision. It is exercised somewhere below the level of consciousness. The result, however, is that the person lays claim to being something he is not. The unconscious nature of that claim makes it acceptable to the claimant— but no less objectionable to the observer.

At times, the kingdom seems crowded with persons whose profession and performance just don't match up. It is this blindness about oneself—this use of denial—that our Lord identified in his message to the church at Laodicea.

"I am rich and well off," you say, "I have all I need." But you do not know how miserable and pitiful you are! You are poor, naked, and blind.
—Revelation 3:17

And the spiritual progeny of the Laodiceans live on!

You have probably noted that to my way of thinking there is a clear difference between hypocrisy and denial. Hypocrisy is a conscious act. The hypocrite is an actor. He knows that the role of goodness he plays is not consistent with his "majority-of-the-time" self. Hypocrites have always taken it on the chin from both religious insiders and outsiders, and they probably deserve the criticism.

Perhaps, though, it's time somebody said a good word for hypocrisy. At least the hypocrite knows his spiritual state is abominable. His acts of hypocrisy—every one of them—are admissions to himself that he is not as good as he ought to be. There is always the possibility that the inner conflict produced by hypocrisy may create enough dissonance, enough discomfort, to move him toward consistency, either for better or for worse. Hypocrisy yields hope for change.

Denial is different! It is an unconscious act. This person feels that whatever behavior he engages in comes from a pure heart. The denying Christian can destroy others—and still feel righteous. His ancestors have stoned and burned and drowned good people in the defense of the faith. He, himself, is still annihilating the dissenters with words and rejection. If you force me to choose between a denier and a hypocrite, I'll go with the hypocrite every time. At least, deep inside, he knows he's not the sort of person he should be. He knows himself.

When the Christian gets to the place of denial,

however, he has obviously arrived at a spiritually unhealthy state. The tragedy is compounded, too, by the fact that because of the unconscious nature of the behavior, it is usually a chronic problem. Denying one's shortcomings prevents the person from doing anything about them. Real spiritual growth—creative and healthy change—cannot take place in the presence of denial.

To employ denial takes a lot of energy, too. Keeping reality from emerging to consciousness is like trying to hold a basketball under water. You can do it—but it takes concentration and energy. One can only wonder how much energy could be released for other purposes if Christians no longer found it necessary to deny their spiritual poverty.

Enough of the problem. It's obvious. What about a solution? There are two basic ways that we can contribute to cutting down on denial (and hypocrisy) and releasing the energy it consumes for constructive service. First, we can change the environment in which we grow Christians. The church, prayer and Bible study groups, even the home, must become places where it is acceptable to be who we are—so long as we are struggling to grow. We can no longer be a part of a system that values professed attainment over obvious struggle; for a Christian who believes he has "arrived" is a glaring contradiction in terms. We are strugglers, pilgrims on a difficult journey. We must not forget that there is virtue in the struggle—whether we are, for the moment, victor or vanquished.

Also, we can come to grips with the fact that even the most compulsive Christian does not have to achieve his goal of total Christlikeness to be comfortable with himself. The fact that our goal is an unattainable one does not consign us to perpetual misery or force us to employ denial.

This good news is contained in two principles—one, psychological, and the other, traditionally religious. These principles are "directionality" and "grace."

In the simplest of terms, the concept of directionality states that tension is experienced by the person who has a goal he has not attained. The tension is reduced, however, by the person's moving toward the identified goal. Conversely, tension builds to a troubling level when the person moves away from his goal. Just moving in the proper direction can keep tension at a healthy level, even if the ultimate goal is never reached.

Translated into the Christian experience, this means that when I go to bed at night, I can rest if I feel that I have made some progress—however slight it may be—toward becoming the kind of person I want to be. I am in trouble, though, and the tension increases disturbingly if I am forced to admit to myself that I am now farther from my goal than when I last checked my position.

It is the principle of "directionality" that the Apostle Paul found in his own experience and described in his letter to the Philippians. "I do not claim that I have already succeeded or have already become perfect . . . the only thing I do, however, is to forget what is behind me and do my best to reach what is ahead. *So I run straight toward the goal. . . .*"

Granting the assumptions that man is a goal-setting organism and that not being at the goal creates tension in the person, it would seem to follow that the person who experiences the discomfort of too much tension would quite naturally be propelled toward the goal. In other words—a believer who has set Christian goals cannot keep from moving toward those goals.

Even a casual look at the human scene, however, discredits such an assumption. Many Christians do successfully escape growth, and they do it either through denial—adapting to the tension and assuming that a guilty conscience is the common lot of believers—or they deal with the tension in ways described by a researcher named Josephine Hilgard.

It was Dr. Hilgard's research that called attention to the fact that the tension produced by the person's having a conscious goal toward which he is not progressing can be reduced in some nonproductive, though not particularly neurotic ways. For instance, she pointed out that a person can reduce that annoying level of tension by making elaborate plans for attaining his goal. How many times have you seen your friends (or yourself) do this? "Someday I am going to (further my education, for instance), and I will go about it in these ways." This was the ploy used by the eager young man who fully intended to become a disciple of Jesus after he had "buried his father."

Hilgard found, too, that just talking about the problem was tension reducing. The troubled person can describe the issue, talk about the personal pain it produces, and feel better as a temporary result.

It appears to me that these rather simple findings provide a potential indictment of a lot of so-called psychotherapy or religious counseling. By providing the troubled person with a continuing forum for making plans and reporting on his miseries, the counselor may be reducing the possibility of growth and change. The counselor, the minister, the friend, or the confidant of any variety, must insist at some point that plans be put into effect and that verbiage is no permanent substitute for progress.

My own history provides an illustration of how one can use evasive and nonproductive ways to deal with the tension that is produced by lack of attainment. For years I have wanted to write. Anyone who does a lot of speaking knows that generally the spoken words are soon gone from the hearer's memory. Since I felt I had some things to say—some things worth being remembered—it seemed a part of my stewardship to write them down. For ten years I've handled the tension in nonproductive ways. First, I reasoned that I had to finish the Ph.D. before I wrote much. "It will give more clout to what I write." Then, seven years ago, with the granting of the Ph.D., that excuse (a plan to begin *after*) wouldn't hold up; so I came up with the idea that I was too busy and usually too tired to be creative. After all, I was in charge of a growing institution—one that teetered at times on the brink of disaster—and it took all I had to give it direction. Then, thank God, after four years of struggle, the Ecumenical Center for Religion and Health came of age. Its programs are strong and its financial base almost secure.

I was running out of ways to plan instead of produce; so I resorted to doing a lot of talking about the guilt I felt about not writing. I laid this load on colleagues—and I really put it on my family. At times, I even spent an hour or two with pen in hand just to prove my good faith. But still I was not writing—at least not much.

Then the crisis came. A person who cares about me, one whose love and motivation I could not question, confronted me. We were sitting at dinner in a lovely place, and Jeanne (my wife) said that the time had come for me to quit talking about it and start writing. She was willing to help, but I had to arrange my schedule, use some self-discipline, and get on the road.

So I'm on that road. I will always have to live with the fact that I'll never achieve all my writing goals. But I'm here to tell you that being on that road toward a goal feels good. It feels a lot better than having to deal with my guilt in nonproductive ways. And it helps me tell my readers that what counts is that you are on the way.

The message is this. Though the Christian is imperfect, he doesn't have to deny the imperfection to be at peace with himself. Just being on the road and moving in the right direction is enough. "Healthy are those who know they are spiritually poor."

For the Christian pilgrim whose goals are always beyond him, there is one other very basic, but profound principle—the principle of God's grace. God has never, and will never, deal with us only on the basis of our goodness or successes.

Our relationship to him began with his forgiveness and continues because he continues to forgive us. That gap between where we are on our pilgrimage and where we should be is always filled by his forgiveness—by his grace.

It's strange to me that many persons who admit that their life in Christ began when they accepted his free forgiveness now seem to feel that they must rely on their own goodness—or their own great strides of spiritual growth—to keep the Father happy with them. Not so. Our relationship with God had its beginning in his grace and continues to rest on that foundation.

We are always being forgiven, and the role of the forgiven keeps us in the posture of gratitude. A daily cure for inordinate pride is a daily expression of gratitude to God for his forgiveness. Remember the story Jesus told Simon the Pharisee? It went something like this: Two men owed the same creditor money. One owed fifty dollars, and the other owed a whopping five hundred dollars. When the notes were due, neither debtor had the resources to pay them off. Try as they would, they couldn't muster the money. Visions of indentured servitude must have been bouncing through their minds when they appeared—empty-handed—before their creditor. But the inexplicable happened. Their creditor tore up the notes—just forgave them their debts. They walked away without the burden of debt or the guilt of failure.

On the basis of this story, Jesus asked Simon a very penetrating question: "Which one of those

forgiven debtors will love his benefactor most?"
The response he made—and the one the Teacher
was going after—was that the one who was
forgiven the most would love the most. Jesus
approved of that answer and suggested that the
Pharisee had inadvertently stated a spiritual
law—a law that explained the difference in the
Pharisee's attitude and the attitude of an ex-whore
toward the Christ. She was freshly forgiven—and
the Pharisee didn't really know what the word
meant. Hers was an emotional relationship with
Christ. His was, at best, formal and cynical.

Many honest churchmen have begun to wonder
how to get some feeling back in the faith. It seems
to them that it has become heavy of head and light
of heart. The answer is clearly set forth in the New
Testament. We must wake up to our spiritual
poverty. We must call for, and be aware of, the
gift of constant grace. Then we will love God as all
forgiven sinners do—with feeling.

I remember an old gospel song that was one of
my father's favorites. It goes like this:

> Naught have I gotten, but what I received
> Grace hath bestowed it since I have believed
> Boasting excluded; pride I abase
> I'm only a sinner, saved by grace.
>
> Suffer that sinner whose heart overflows
> Loving his Savior, to tell what he knows.
> Once more to tell it, would I embrace
> I'm only a sinner—saved by grace.

—D. B. Towner

As a child, hearing my father sing this song and talk about the beauty and meaning of it did nothing for me. He was the straightest, most moral man I have ever known. I didn't know what "grace" meant—and I certainly didn't know what he meant when he talked about it. Now I think I know. I know that grace means an undeserved gift—and I know that my father felt he had needed it and received it. Good as he was, he was painfully aware of the gap that existed between who and where he was and who and where he should be. And it was his knowledge of the forgiveness of God that made that gap bearable. He was, after all was said and done, a sinner saved, not by his goodness, but by God's grace. He was a pilgrim on a journey, and he had a long way to go. But the distance between him and the goal was filled completely by the grace of God.

"Healthy are those who know they are forgiven strugglers."

THREE
The Mourning Christian

*"Happy are
those who mourn . . ."* ❧

Wouldn't it be interesting to know how many casual readers of the New Testament have been turned off by reading the second beatitude? Who wants to be blessed by mourning—and what does "happy are those who mourn" mean? It would seem to suggest that my future joy is to be measured out in direct proportion to my present misery. This approach might even tempt one to create temporal misery so that he can experience eternal joy. This is a serious perversion of the Teacher's message! It is this kind of blurred interpretation of Christ's teaching, however, that has spawned all sorts of atrocities—and created a bovine acceptance of the miserable status quo in generations of Christians.

Generations of slaves marched to the fields thinking that their servitude and suffering were ordained by God and that he would compensate them for their pain in another life. Others have bought the idea that the Christian life is divinely designed to be heavy and joyless—and happiness is reserved for eternity. For these, any claim to present joy is a rebellion against the plan and purposes of God. Death, for them, is the only avenue to freedom and joy.

The Sermon on the Mount, however, does not present a sweet-by-and-by philosophy. It is very much tied to the now-and-now. So at this point, the term "healthy" has special meaning as a substitute adjective for blessed or happy. It gives it a contemporary flavor!

Remember—Jesus was talking to people who lost a lot when they decided to follow him. They were called away from family, traditional religion, their closest friends, and, in many instances, their business or profession. Later, some would face martyrdom. When they chose to follow Jesus, most that was old and familiar had to be discarded. Their families did not understand their new allegiance, and they became strangers among their kin. Their friends were bewildered and alienated by their new faith. The comforting rituals of traditional religion were no longer a part of their life style, and the emerging new methods of faith's expression were not yet clearly defined. These people had experienced significant losses, and they needed help. It has never been enough to remind a person of how much he gains when he seems to lose. There still is loss—and every loss needs to be mourned.

The church has been slow to accept this teaching about mourning and health. We have been guilty of transmitting the message that "big Christians don't cry"—or at least do not admit that they do. Only very recently have we begun to realize that to deny grief is to deny a natural human function and that such denial sometimes produces dire consequences. Grief, like any genuine emotion, is accompanied by certain physical changes and the release of a form of psychic energy. If that energy is not expended in the normal processes of grieving, it becomes destructive within the person. Usually, depression will set in. At times angry, inappropriate behavior toward those closest to the person will be substituted. You can't just ignore a sense of loss and expect it to go away!

Even physical illness can be a penalty for unresolved grief. Researchers have begun to call attention to the physical vulnerability of persons who have suffered a significant loss. More specifically, it has been noted that a disproportionate number of widows or widowers contract a serious or fatal illness within two years of their mate's death. Is this the physical price paid for improper grieving? Students of human behavior are beginning to believe that this is the case.

Then there is that specter of depression that often follows a loss. Depression differs from grief in that it (depression) is chronic and does not readily present a cause for the sadness. Grieving is a process—one with definable and predictable stages through which one moves. It also has an object. A person grieves over a specific loss. Deep depression, however, is an illness which often can be lifted only with the use of extraordinary measures such as extended psychotherapy, mood elevating drugs, or even electroconvulsive therapy.

There are reams yet to be written about depression—the classic late twentieth-century illness of the middle class and middle aged. For now, though, let's leave it by saying it is an illness that, like other forms of disease, can be produced by improper grieving. Credit Jesus with another scientifically confirmed insight 2000 years ahead of its time when he told his followers that mourning was related to health.

Let me illustrate the relationship between mourning and health with Carol's story. She was an attractive, bright, middle-aged lady who came to see me with the familiar story of real depression. She had a job but didn't enjoy it. Sometimes she felt she wasn't doing well at work. Her memory was bad and her efficiency seemed impaired. She reported that she had no social life—and really hadn't the energy to try to create social contacts. Her nonworking hours were spent alone. She cried a lot, sometimes for no apparent reason, and wondered if people were beginning to think her strange. The lights had gone out for Carol. She felt alone, afraid, tired, and without hope. It was a kind of survival reflex that had brought her for therapy.

We hadn't probed far into her social and family history until an obvious cause for her depression grabbed me. Within a period of two years, Carol had lost every significant male in her life. Her father died unexpectedly of a heart attack. Her husband contracted cancer and was gone in a matter of a few months. Then her only son—a bright and promising graduate student—was found to have a brain tumor. Quickly, he, too, was gone.

This history of tragic loss moved me deeply; so I was intrigued by the matter-of-fact way that my new friend recited the stories of these losses. The next question followed quite naturally. "Carol, how did you take these deaths?" She smiled a rather tight smile and said, "All of my friends told me I did beautifully. I remember telling myself that I had to be strong for my mother. To tell the truth, I was deeply hurt, but I hardly cried." There it was. Two or three years had passed. Years of pushing aside memories and running from pain. But she had lost the battle. Unresolved grief had yielded to deep depression.

Carol's therapy was not difficult to design. She went back to the losses and got in touch with the pain and the anger. She cried a lot and talked bitterly of the injustice of it all. When the process was over, she was better. She is now a productive employee who is active in the community. And she laughs a lot. There are still those moments of sadness, often near the anniversary of one of those losses, but the depression has gone. Carol found that grief cannot be denied, it can only be delayed—and the delay can be costly.

So far, we have talked about the great big losses of our lives and our reaction to them. I doubt that more needs to be said about these. We will handle them when they come. We won't welcome them, but we will mourn them and find the predictable course of our grieving somewhat lightened by our hope. There is a touch of the hero in each of us. At times we have even rehearsed in our minds our heroic responses to great tragedies. We will make it through them.

The rub often comes at the point of the little tragedies—the less-than-notable losses. I once heard someone say that most Christians deal better with death than with burned cakes. An exaggeration, perhaps, but one grown from a kernel of truth.

It may very well be that these little, everyday, unadmitted and unmourned losses contribute to a Christian's poor health. It may even be that these little losses, in aggregate, comprise a heavy burden for some of God's children. Our incomplete mourning builds up on us like barnacles on a ship, and as barnacles slow the ship, our unfinished mourning keeps us from our maximum efficiency and health.

What are these small, unmourned losses? The truth is that many of them seem very pedestrian—unworthy of being mourned—but they are not insignificant. The fact that you seldom experience change without experiencing a loss may make a loss commonplace—but not insignificant. Even though you welcome the change, the commensurate loss can make it a mixed blessing.

Remember when you got that new house or that new car? Most have experienced a tinge of sadness when they walked through the old, well-lived-in house for the last time. Leaving the battered and out-dated automobile on the lot felt strange, too. Something that was yours and with which you associate a lot of memories would now belong to a stranger.

Move on up the scale of loss and think of your feelings when a child left home for the first time. He needed to go. That's what families are about, raising adults who can leave home without feeling guilty and live constructively outside that protective environment. When he left, there was a sense of accomplishment—but weren't there some tears, too?

Some of us periodically are grabbed by the sense of a lost past—a lost youth. We look in the mirror. The wrinkles are there, the hair has changed color like the leaves of autumn. Body contours are subtly changing. We become aware that there is not quite as much available energy as there once was.

Lost friends, lost health, lost jobs, lost opportunity, lost innocence, lost dreams—the list goes on and on. The longer one lives, the longer the personal list of losses. The world is filled with reminders. The face of a stranger reminds you of a dead friend. A place calls to your mind a lost opportunity. A song makes you remember a lost childhood. If most of the items represent a piece of unfinished mourning, it is no small wonder that many experience a decline of mental health as aging takes place.

The message is this. Any event, any awareness that contains a sense of loss for you can, and should, be mourned. This doesn't mean a life of incessant sadness. It means being willing to admit to an honest feeling rather than always having to laugh off the pain. It's not only permissible to admit the sadness that accompanies any loss—it's the healthy option. Stay current with your mourning.

Our problem with mourning points to the broader truth that many Christians have a lot of trouble dealing with some emotions. The tendency seems to be to view the emotions as though they were based on a good-bad continuum. In other words, some emotions are good and deserve full expression. Others are bad—and ought never to be expressed. This attitude allows—even encourages—the feeling and expression of emotions such as joy and love, but it causes the person to keep the wraps on such emotions as anger, grief, and despair.

But Jesus acknowledged the need to express those supposedly darker emotions. He not only gave verbal approval—he expressed these emotions himself. He was angry with those who represented the religious establishment, and had some not-too-complimentary things to say to them. He was more than "upset" by the misuse of his Father's house and expressed his anger directly when he drove the money-changers out. Can we forget his weeping over a dead friend and sharing the mourning of the people of Bethany? Doesn't the picture of his tears on the hilltop overlooking the unbelieving population of Jerusalem live in our minds? He was, indeed, a man of sorrows and acquainted with grief—and he expressed his sorrows with tears.

Part of the Good News, both stated and lived by the Carpenter, is that a proper expression of all emotions has divine approval. The key is "proper expression." The scriptural injunctions are "be angry—and sin not," "sorrow, but not as those who have no hope." Our very human and very necessary emotions must be expressed, but they should always be filtered through a Christian value system. The expression of emotions will keep them from damaging us; and filtering them through Christian values will keep their expression from damaging others.

The alternative to feeling and expressing the full range of human emotions is what psychologists call a "flattened effect"—or what others might label the "personality blahs." I am convinced that you can't repress a *few* emotions without inhibiting your ability to feel and express *all* emotions. The person who will not tune in to his sadness—his mourning—will not be able to feel the complete range of his joy. The person who denies his anger may find it difficult to feel and express his love.

So, in encouraging us to mourn, Jesus opens up the full range of our humanity. He lets us come out of the closet with our sadness and our anger. "Healthy are those who mourn" cuts us loose from the "giggle your way to glory" crowd. The polar extremes of my feelings are liberated. I am a mourner—and an ecstatic rejoicer. I am angry—and I am filled with love. And in these polar extremes, I am most human—and could it be, most Christian?

"Healthy are those who are able to express constructively the full range of their emotions."

FOUR
The
Teachable
Christian

*"Happy are
the meek . . ."* ❧

Have you ever noticed that you like some words and dislike others? How do you feel about words like "cancer," "dirty," "lonely," and "odor"—or "love," "beauty," "peace," and "home"? The reason for our emotional reactions to words is that some of them carry two kinds of meaning for us. Every word has a denotative meaning—the dictionary definition. Some words, though, also have connotative meaning. The appearance or sound of the word creates an emotional response in us.

I know, of course, that "meek" is a perfectly good English word meaning "gentle and patient." That's what Webster says, and he must be correct. But the word "meek" calls out an emotional response in me. I don't like the word. It seems to convey an attitude of subservience—a doormat kind of existence. When I hear the word I think of Casper Milquetoast, the comic strip character who was intimidated by everyone and everything around him. I don't want to be like him—and surely Jesus is not telling me to be.

In order to give this beatitude a positive meaning for me, I went in search of a synonym. I wanted a word that would carry what I feel to be the depth of meaning in this beatitude without arousing negative emotions in me and some of my friends. I tried "humble"—and found, somewhat to my surprise and embarrassment, that it left me with negative feelings, too. Perhaps I have known too many people who have flaunted their humility, and this didn't quite compute for me. They announced their humility and were proud of it. Somehow, "humility" has gotten associated with professing not to care for oneself. Also, there is a strong contradiction in being told to strive for humility. Would I recognize it when I had attained it? And would knowing I was humble quickly destroy its reality for me? No, "humble" was not the word I was looking for.

I came upon my synonym in a most unexpected place. Every fall I take a teaching assignment with the Department of Psychiatry at the University of Texas Medical School at San Antonio. The class has put me in close contact with some second year medical students and has been a learning experience for me. The teaching takes place in a nontraditional way. The entire second year class meets for a lecture, and then is broken into units of four. A psychiatrist and a psychologist are assigned to each unit. The task is to teach these students interviewing skills and help them put into practice what they have learned from lectures and books by beginning to deal with psychiatric diagnoses. The students interview patients, write mental status exam reports, and arrive at tentative diagnoses of the patients' illnesses. Watching these students mature and gain confidence is an interesting process.

The problem with this course—at least from the teacher's standpoint—is that each student must be given a numerical grade at the end of the course. For the most part, the grade is the product of the combined subjective judgments of the two teachers, which is not the best grading method in the world, I'm afraid.

It was at a session in which the co-teacher and I were assigning grades that I found my word. We had gone through the names of the students in both groups that we taught, and strangely enough, were in almost perfect agreement about their grades. All passed—but a few seemed to us to deserve high marks. The assigned grades were, quite obviously, out of proportion to the students' interviewing and diagnostic abilities. These skills still needed some sharpening. Why were we grading a few so highly, then? We searched for the reason and finally agreed that it was "teachableness" to which we were responding so positively.

Some students had come into our class with a bored, I'm-doing-you-a-favor-by-being-here attitude. Others came like sponges. They soaked up all you gave—and asked for more. They had the attitude that I hope my doctor had when he was in medical school—and still has. They were teachable. They learned.

For me the word "teachable" fits this beatitude! It's the synonym I was looking for.

It fits what I hear Jesus saying time and again. "Follow me and I will make you become . . ." or "Take my yoke upon you and learn of me." He was the traveling teacher calling people to sign on as learners. The teachable heard him.

It fits what I sense beneath the pages of the Gospels as the state of mind that motivated a few to follow Jesus. There was a sense of dissatisfaction with this life. What they had learned about living wasn't working. There were too many rules, too much pain, too much loneliness, too little meaning, too little love, and not enough sense of belonging. They were ready to learn a new life style. For them, it was leaving time—and learning time. Out of their desperation, they had become teachable.

It fits the terminology of the epistles. John, in particular, addresses the Christians as "little children." It is the child—and the child in each of us—that is beautifully open to receive new knowledge. Closed-mindedness and satisfaction with what we already know is a condition of grown-ups.

It fits my experience. In those moments when I feel most alive and most healthy, I have been ready to learn. It may even be that a willingness to learn creates a sense of vitality and hope. Whatever the sequence, it is true for me. To be healthy is to be learning.

Mark me down as a person who envies the earliest Christians. Their path was more individual—far less institutionalized than ours. There was so much to be learned about this new Christian life style. Few persons had walked the way before them and charted a course. These early disciples were stretched to find how their faith should cause them to relate to the world.

Now much learning comes in large chunks for the little children of the kingdom. By joining a fellowship of Christians—a church—they quickly commit themselves to a traditional way of expressing faith and living in the world. They now spend time learning what they are supposed to know and how they are supposed to behave in order to be good Baptists, Episcopalians, Roman Catholics, or what have you. Some of the excitement of the laboratory kind of living is gone—replaced by a history lesson. It's not that we need to scrap tradition and all it teaches us. Learning from the past is one of those qualities that distinguishes man from the lower animals. The issue is that we must release the teachable to learn more than the past can teach them. To do this, the organized structures of the faith are going to have to become genuinely tolerant of the eager and honest Christians who push the perimeters of accepted life style and ask challenging questions about the faith. These may be the healthiest ones among us.

Let me go back for a minute to the little child analogy. Of such, you know, is the kingdom of heaven. It appears to me that one of our goals—both for ourselves and those we love—should be to preserve a childlike quality of life. A number of years ago, I was deeply moved by a picture that accompanied a brief essay on childhood. (Frankly, the picture had more to say than the written essay.) It was the picture of a child, probably aged seven or eight, staring intently into a mud puddle. He was seeing fascinating things in that puddle, and the whole world could go on by while he took it in. The picture moved me because it was a graphic reminder of how aloof from the ordinary I had become and how difficult it was for me to learn. I vowed, as I viewed that picture, to try to be more aware of mud puddles of all kinds; to try to remain curious about the ordinary; to try to be open to experiencing and learning little things.

I'm not sure that I have even come close to

keeping my vow. It's hard for me. My family, my upwardly mobile friends, my professors, and yes, my church have programmed me to be taught only by the extraordinary and to listen only to the instruction of the giants. I'll keep on trying—but it would have been far better if those persons and institutions closest to me had dealt more kindly with my childlike teachableness when I first entered the kingdom.

There's a whole book to be written about how our world treats teachableness. To some the teachable person is gullible—too open and too easily fooled. To others, he is perceived as weak. He is not positive and judgmental enough. To still others he is a threat. The status quo is not quite enough for him, and this makes him difficult to predict or control. The world—even the church part of it—is far more comfortable with persons whose minds are made up.

Twenty years ago I walked in friendship for a few brief and special years with a genuinely intellectually curious person. He was a fellow minister—a man of faith—for whom old stereotyped answers would not do.

I have vivid memories of a night when our conversation lasted until dawn. It seemed to me that my friend was attacking my faith. He asked questions I didn't want to hear, let alone try to answer. Because my answers were weak and I felt threatened, I became angry. How dare anyone— especially a true friend—ask those questions and then shoot holes in the answers I had learned from pious people, I thought. It was a difficult night for me! I can report, though, that I began right then to strengthen some intellectual and spiritual muscles that up to that time had been unexercised.

I want to underline the fact that my friend's questions did not come because he did not have faith. They came because he did have faith, and he wanted that faith to be personal, tough, and related to the present. He was bright and he was teachable. And he dared to have questions and to voice them, not just to shock his friends, but in hopes of hearing relevant answers. He is a special person to whom I will always be indebted.

If you asked where he is now and what he is doing with his life, I would have to tell you that I am not sure. This I do know, though. He is no longer officially connected to the church. I'm confident that he attends worship services, and I know he is still a man of faith. But the church couldn't seem to deal with his questioning nature, and both he and the church were losers.

This is not to say that the teachable Christian is a person with a mind like a sieve. There are some things about which he has made up his mind. He has taken what Kierkegaard called the "leap of faith." He has staked his life, his eternity, on his commitment to the idea that God is—and that God "was in Christ reconciling the world unto himself." He has embraced the Scriptures as truth. Where the Bible speaks, he is ready to listen to it as truth. But just as important, he is ready to be silent where the Scriptures are silent.

As I write this chapter, I am traveling home from a visit to my physical roots. I have spent some days with my mother and have worshiped with people who knew me as a boy. I found that these friends from my childhood and I share a commitment to Jesus Christ, but some of our other values are poles apart. On this journey, I went back to a negative view of the Christian life. I listened to sermons that spoke more of God's judgment than his grace. I spent time with my brother who long ago was turned off to God by the people of God. Strong, mixed feelings are emerging to consciousness. There is a feeling of gratitude for parents and friends who introduced me to God and have prayed so often for me. There is some anger, too, incited by what I believe to be their religious bigotry. And there is that strange feeling of alienation. I am no longer where I was and where they still seem to be.

I would like to believe that the difference has been created by my growth—a growth spawned by teachableness. I know they would say that I have wandered from my faith. Their judgment and their lack of understanding bring me pain. But I cannot go back. There is too much joy, too much excitement in who I have become. And, just maybe, there is health, too.

"Healthy are those who are eager and able to learn."

FIVE
The Trusting Christian

*"Happy are those
whose greatest desire
is to do
what God requires . . ."* ❧

The *Good News for Modern Man* translation of the fourth beatitude came as a shock to me. "Happy is the man whose greatest desire is to do what God requires" can pose a problem for a veteran of many serious and time-consuming "will of God" discussions.

As a young student and then a young minister, I have talked away a lot of hours in discussions about how one comes to know God's will. As I think back, it now seems to me that two assumptions—both of them wrong—formed the foundation on which these arguments were constructed. First, there was the idea that "discovering" the will of God was difficult. God was being coy with us, and only the most insistent and pious ones of us would get the word from him.

Then there was the idea that when we finally got the word, it would be bad news. God's will was always tough and would inevitably demand great personal sacrifice. Usually, of course, it involved "surrendering" to something—a term not too appealing to most of us. ("Surrender" seemed to go quite naturally with "mission field" and "preach.") In support of this assumption, I have heard scores of persons tell how God tortured them into finally giving in to his call.

Somehow, you see, early in my life the will of God became associated with the sacrifice of my will—even the sacrifice of myself. Wanting to do the will of God might be the mark of the deeply religious, but to make it a characteristic of the happy and healthy didn't fit my concept of that will.

Now I read that Jesus said the healthy disciple passionately desires to do the will of God. This didn't match up with my concept of the result of doing God's will and the kinds of persons who were searching for that will. It is precisely this kind of incongruity that has often led to growth for me. What I had come to believe and what the Scriptures were saying were in conflict. Either I could rationalize my way around this statement about the will of God, or I could reexamine my belief. In this instance, I chose reexamination.

Slowly, it began to dawn on me that my reluctance about looking for God's place for me was rooted in an incorrect, inadequate, and childish concept of God. I saw him as angry and his behavior toward me as basically punitive. I could not trust him to do right by me. As strange as it seems, I supposedly had trusted God with my eternal life but was afraid to trust him with my mortal life.

How does an adult wind up with an inadequate and limiting concept of God? Usually, it's because we have entered adulthood with ideas about God that seemed to serve us well in childhood. The problem is that childish ideas about God and spiritual growth just don't go together. Those who study the child's concept of God tell me that because of the undeveloped state of the child's intellect, he must view God in very concrete terms. The idea of the spiritual nature of the Father may be difficult for some adults—but it is impossible for children. Somehow, the child's God is always a big, strong person—a bigger, stronger version of his earthly father. After all, he is taught to call God "Father"; so the association between the father he sees and knows and the One he cannot see is formed. (There is a lot to be written about the responsibility this places on Dad, but that will have to wait.)

It's easy to see that the child with a warm, loving, expressive, and strong father will have that kind of God to rely on. On the other hand, the child whose father is distant and frightening will have that kind of heavenly Father. Not many generations ago the dominant American parenting style was to transmit warmth, acceptance, and advocacy to the children through the mother. Dad was the provider—and usually the distant, disciplining patriarch. So the children of those generations grew up and emphasized in their thinking, teaching, and preaching the sternness and anger of God. Now the parenting styles in our country have begun to change. In many families, Dad has been liberated to be warm and overtly loving—and the chore of discipline is shared by both parents. The children produced by these families have different ideas about God. For them, he may not even be stern enough to fit the biblical descriptions.

The issue is that whatever the child's concept of God, it is simply that—a child's concept. It does not do justice to God or to the mature intellect. If one is to grow up spiritually, he must allow his ideas about God to change. He must come to view the Father more in terms of the Incarnation than in terms of his earthly father. Jesus showed us God as he is and wants to be known. While the total being of God is more than could be revealed in Jesus, this is the best image that a person can gain of the true nature of the heavenly Father. Being sensitive to what God shows and tells us about himself in Jesus Christ inevitably brings about a shift in our God-concept. It gets us ready to make mature responses to God.

As my concept of God began to shift, my ideas about the will of God began to change. Accepting the fact (not just the words) that God loves me and wills the best for me was step one. Recognizing that all of this good that he wanted for me was not reserved for eternity was step two. Discovering that God recognizes, honors, and uses my uniqueness was step three. When I put all of this together, the will of God was no longer something to be surrendered to. It became an exciting program of personal happiness and usefulness to get plugged into. Everybody talks about personal fulfillment these days. Can't this be a synonym for doing the Father's will?

This beatitude suggests, too, that there should be a feeling of urgency about getting plugged into God's place for us. Hunger and thirst (the wording of the King James Version) speak of basic drives—those that sustain life. Our adventures with the will of God, in the same manner, sustain spiritual vitality. Many bored and listless Christians erroneously think that

God has handed them a detailed road map that pretty well orders their pilgrimage from the point of commitment to doing his will until death. All they can do is trudge along doing the same chore in the same way until death relieves them.

This is a tragic interpretation of God's will and his call. No wonder those who interpret God's will in this way dread doing it! The fact is that his leadership today is much as it was for the wandering Israelites—a moment at a time. They followed the cloud by day and the fire by night. They knew the destination—God had shared that with them—but they had to trust him for the route. The fascinating new directions in which he leads us keep us alive. We should never be certain what we and God will be doing the day after tomorrow.

This concept of the dynamic nature of the will of God makes many people nervous. Family, close friends, and church are usually most comfortable when we are traditional and predictable. Although lip service is paid to the idea that well-meaning Christians want each other to be sensitive to the present will of God, great consternation is expressed when a lawyer is led away from the practice of law or a minister feels drawn to some untraditional ministry.

It has been six years now since the direction of my own ministry changed. For twenty years I was a traditional pastor and preacher. When I became a teacher and counselor in an institution other than the local church, all sorts of criticism were launched and strange inferences were drawn.

It's a story that has been repeated in some form dozens of times over the past six years, but I remember one particular encounter very well. I had been preaching on several consecutive Sundays in a church that was pastorless. As I stood at the door after the service to greet the worshipers (a behavior on the part of ministers that I do not quite understand), a well-dressed woman who appeared to be in her sixties stood off to the side, quite obviously waiting for an opportunity to speak with me. When most of the people had gone, she stepped up and extended her hand. Looking directly at me, she said, "Every time I hear you preach, it makes me sad."

What's the proper response to that kind of opening statement? "Thank you, I appreciate that," just doesn't seem to fill the bill. All I could think to do was to say, "I'm sorry. Would you mind sharing with me what it is about my preaching that makes you sad?"

"Oh, it's not the way you preach or what you say that saddens me," she said. "What makes me sad is that you have chosen to leave the ministry. The church needs preachers like you."

"Then let me deal with your sadness," I told her. "I haven't left the ministry. My ministry has only taken on a new direction. I still preach, teach, and counsel—only in a less traditional setting."

"But you don't have a church," she argued, "and it's such a waste."

I tried hard to explain—but she never got the message. For her, the will of God for a minister was stereotyped. I didn't fit the mold; so, I was not a minister. She will be sad the next time she hears me, too.

I wish I knew how many times I have been asked why I left the ministry. Most of the inquirers didn't seem to understand when I responded that I had not left the ministry, but had just found the shape of my ministry for the present. I wish I could convey to them the excitement and sense of adventure I experienced when the direction of my service changed.

In the last few years, a lot of books have hit the market that describe the doldrums of the middle years. Most of them recommend that the bored "middlescent" be open to the possibility of change. To be able to consider a change of direction lifts the smog of despair. If the person chooses to continue his present life style, at least he has done it by choice, not by default. If he chooses to change, he may enter the new role with youthful vigor. Bookshelves are studded with the biographies of persons whose greatest contribution was made at an age when most of their peers were coasting toward idleness. They escaped the rut and really produced.

The idea of the dynamic will of God meets the need of many. God does not want his children to be burdened and blunted by stultifying sameness. He wants life to be an adventure, and he wants us constantly to check our personal cloud and pillar of fire for a possible change of direction.

"Healthy is the person whose greatest desire is to do the will of God"; for God will keep him alive and excited.

Health is reflected in wanting to do God's will for another reason, too. In order to want desperately to do his will, you have to have—not just an adult concept of God—but a *healthy* adult concept. This will relate not only to the specific issue of your calling but to your total being. An angry, punitive God will make life tough for you if you listen to him and follow his leadership. Only a God of love and a Father who wills us peace and joy can be trusted to the point of our really wanting what he wants for us. The person who feels driven to do the will of God is a person who has a healthy concept of God.

Mental illness sometimes involves a distorted concept of God. Fears, obsessions, and guilt abound in the pitiable Christian with an angry heavenly Father. For that person, living is like walking through a mine field. He is almost afraid to move because the next step may be a wrong one and—boom! So the frightened Christian tiptoes through life in constant fear of setting off a demonstration of the anger of God. He is afraid that if he steps wrong, God will "get him."

On the other hand, to have God on your side helps you to live courageously and healthily. You may step wrong and fail miserably—but

70

God will come to rescue you, not destroy you. Knowing that God is our friend and not our adversary nudges us toward health—and the healthy Christian can fearlessly seek the will of God.

"Healthy are those whose concept of God is so positive that they can want to do his will."

SIX
*The
Forgiving
Christian*

*"Happy are those
who are merciful   ஐ
to others . . ."*

Jesus was a revolutionary—and seldom is that fact more clearly demonstrated than when he talked about the way the healthy Christian relates to others. What he has already said about the intrapersonal qualities of the healthy disciple is shocking enough—but he lets out all the stops on the subject of interpersonal relationships.

The people around Jesus were well schooled in the techniques of dealing with others. Justice was the key word. When treated well, you were to treat the person well in return. When wronged, you could exact the price of that wrong. The Teacher put it like this, "You have heard that it was said, 'An eye for an eye, and a tooth for a tooth . . .' " Yes, they had heard it, and from the most credible of persons—their parents and religious leaders. Sure, they had gotten the message of justice, and something within them—as within all of us—had said it was right. This is the way the world should be run. The "get even" mentality had become a part of them as it becomes a part of most of us early in our lives. It is a combination of our survival and our aggressive drives.

So Jesus struck at the very core of who we are when he changed the basic rule about interpersonal relationships from justice to mercy—one of those words that sounds so great and is so hard to practice. He demanded mercy—that act that feels so good and so right when we receive it and so impossible and undeserved when we're called on to give it.

But aren't we back to a familiar concept—the

concept of grace? In the first beatitude we were enjoined to admit our spiritual poverty. This admission threw us on the mercy of a forgiving Father. We are relieved to know that God treats us mercifully—not justly. We are "saved by grace" and often become misty-eyed talking or singing about it. The stinger is, though, that this fifth beatitude does not comfort us with his gift of grace. It suggests, instead, that we become givers of grace. Jesus said it in another context, but it is no less applicable here. "Freely you have received, freely give."

We are dealing, then, with two very basic and interrelated concepts. First, my relationship to God is a product of his forgiveness, not of my goodness. Second, my continuing and constructive relationships with others are based more on my forgiveness than on their goodness. One of the behaviors you can predict in the God of the universe is that he will forgive those who ask him. And a behavior you can predict in the healthy Christian is that he will forgive others even as he has been forgiven by God.

This association between being forgiven and being forgiving is a recurring theme in the teachings of Jesus. In calling us to love each other, he calls us not so much to an emotion as to a principle. The part of that principle which undergirds our relationships is forgiveness; for that is the nature of love. In urging his followers to become as little children, Jesus presses us toward a forgiving attitude. Forgiving is a part of the very nature of a child. Seldom, though, does Jesus state it more explicitly than in the

Lord's Prayer. "Forgive us our trespasses as we forgive those who trespass against us."

Again, to the behavioral scientist, Jesus seems centuries ahead of his time. It is almost axiomatic with students of human behavior that mentally healthy people have good constructive relationships. On the other side of the coin, the mental health professional sees disrupted, strained relationships as a possible indicator of emotional distress or illness.

As a person moves toward identifiable mental illness, he is progressively socially isolated. It seems to him that people can't be trusted. He feels he is the victim of incessant injustice. For that person, the way to survive is to keep his distance from others and be on constant guard against attack. In some cases, it might be that he is just too tired, too emotionally exhausted, to maintain contact with much of the outside world. Whatever the cause, he is walled off from others. He is alone.

If the result of a deteriorating mental state is poor relationships, one has to entertain the possibility that a person's inability to maintain strong, supportive friendships can also be a cause of emotional distress. There is a preventive component in strong relationships. Without our friends, more of us would be found in the mentally unhealthy segment of our society. Unforgiveness, and resulting alienation, will inevitably exact its toll on the person because it has isolated him from others and from God.

Let me illustrate. My father once repeated to

me a story told him by a minister colleague. It seems that a parishioner of this colleague, a woman in her middle years, came to talk with the minister about a spiritual problem. She felt she could no longer pray and be heard. She also reported that she was depressed—and the depression was deepening. The minister-counselor listened carefully to her story and suggested that they begin to work on the obviously spiritual part of her problem—her inability to pray.

"This is fine, pastor, but what are we to do about this? I've prayed and prayed—and I feel that God is a million miles away and that he is choosing not to hear me."

His reply was to request that they pray together. He would pray a phrase and she was to repeat it after him if she could tell God this and mean it. She agreed.

The prayer therapy began. "Our Father, who art in Heaven, hallowed be Thy name"—and she softly echoed the words. On through the Lord's Prayer they moved, phrase stated and phrase repeated, until the minister said, "Forgive us our trespasses as we forgive those who trespass against us." Following this, there was no echo—only heavy silence.

Sensing that the prayer time was over, the minister lifted his head and looked into his parishioner's eyes. Those eyes glinted with memory and anger as she said, "I couldn't say that part of the prayer because I will not—I simply will not—forgive that woman for what she has done to me and my family."

The problem—at least in part—had been identified. Gently, but firmly, the minister told the woman that until she could begin to forgive, she would find it hard to pray. And a kibitzing psychologist could have said that until she could deal constructively with her anger, she would continue to be depressed.

Right at the crux of the issue of forgiveness (mercy) and mental health is the fact that once you perceive that you have been wronged by another person, there are only two responses available to you—anger (my mother's word for it is "hurt") or forgiveness. Or perhaps it's even simpler than that. The first and very human response always is anger and that is followed by the decision of what to do with the anger. Anger is an emotion over which I have little, if any, control. Control is at the level of how I choose to express it—how I choose to use the energy the anger has produced.

It is not the purpose of this chapter to deal with ways to handle anger, except at the most basic level. In simple terms, all our options of how to "get anger out of our system" are subsumed under two headings—constructive and destructive. Anger can be turned toward the destruction of the offending person (and often is), and anger can be turned in on oneself and produce a slow destruction of the person through guilt and depression. Psychoanalytically oriented therapists have long talked about depression as "anger turned inward."

Jesus taught a constructive method of dealing with our sense of being wronged and with the ensuing anger. I like to call it "active forgiveness." Too many people have tried to tell us that Jesus' way to deal with personal hurt and injustice is a kind of bovine acceptance of it. "Go through life expecting to be mistreated and planning to do nothing about it" seems to be the Christian message for many. In support of this theory, they often quote the "second mile" and "turned cheek" parts of the Sermon on the Mount.

I can't buy that as a healthy way to deal with my personal hurts. Repressed anger makes one emotionally ill. Surely Jesus is not laying a load of depression on me by urging this style of life!

It is this very life style heresy that makes many of our great Christians so vulnerable to depression. Time and again I've seen it—persons whose depression shocked me, because they seemed so close to God and so active in his work. In treating them, I have found in a high percentage of cases that they have never learned to deal actively with their anger. They deny their anger, or they repress it. But they do not let it move them to action.

What, then, is "active forgiveness"? Jesus instructed his disciples to tell each other when they felt wronged. "Leave your gift, then, in front of the altar and go at once and make peace with your brother; then come back and offer your gift to God." He didn't want the fellowship in his family disrupted, and he didn't want his children depressed!

But what about the second mile and the turned cheek? First of all, remember that the

Teacher was giving strategies in dealing with the enemy when he gave these instructions. The Christians have already been told to talk with those who offend them—to get it out and forgive. How to deal with those who don't play by Christian rules and against whom you are practically powerless—that's the issue. He (the Teacher) still recommends a form of "active forgiveness." To be forced to carry a soldier's pack for one mile can be humiliating. You are doing what he can force you to do. But carrying it a second mile changes the locus of control from him to you. You walk away from the second mile of pack-bearing feeling like a person. You would have walked away from the first mile feeling like a slave. This is "active forgiveness." You are meeting your needs as well as complying and forgiving.

The key is that in any exercise of "active forgiveness," the forgiver gets his needs met, too. Jesus loves both persons and he will not sacrifice one to the other!

Because the mind-set of the average contemporary American causes him to look into his past to explain his present feelings and behavior, one other form of mercy needs to be presented. It is the merciful treatment of one's parents and other significant people in one's past.

A person who has not forgiven his parents is not a healthy person. Oh, you can trace the historical roots of your unpleasant feelings. You can even—in our society—dump a certain measure of blame on your ancestors. But a person is mature only when he is willing to forgive his parents for their mistakes (even if it has to be on a daily basis), and assume full present responsibility for who he is, how he feels, and what he does. "My parents made me do it!" is not an adequate explanation for feelings and behavior of healthy Christian grownups. Most of us find things wrong with the way we were parented. All of us realize that we have sometimes been victimized by our friends. The healthy ones among us leave these sins in the forgiven past.

So here we stand—called to receive mercy and to be merciful; summoned to grace and to graciousness. This is the foundation of our faith and our Christian fellowship. Without mercy we are neither Christian nor healthy.

"Healthy are those who show mercy to others."

SEVEN
The Honest Christian

*"Happy are
the pure in heart . . ."* ❧

Frankly, this statement of Jesus, "Happy are the pure in heart," is one reason I waited so long to write about the beatitudes.

Early in my ministry, I was very impressed by a book written by the late W. E. Sangster, a great British Methodist minister and writer. It was a book on the beatitudes, but it homed in on the "pure in heart." His thesis was that this was a quality of life possessed by the greatest saints, and by them alone. In this beautiful book, Sangster equated purity of heart with a kind of holy naivete that seemed so far removed from life in the twentieth century that it presented a strange, though intriguing, model for modern man. It was a component of a life style well suited to the first few centuries after Christ and difficult—if not impossible—to achieve in our times. This interpretation of "pure in heart" became part of the mystique surrounding these statements of Christ that seemed to me to put them out of the realm of the relevant for his modern followers.

Slowly it dawned on me that the position of this beatitude among the others had real significance. It was not a part of those statements that dealt with the intrapersonal attributes of the healthy follower of the Way. Instead, it was in the section that talked about interpersonal relationships. Could it be that Jesus was talking about my style of relating to others instead of an ethereal inner quality that set me apart from the masses? For me, the answer was a resounding "yes!" Purity of heart speaks about the way I relate to others and not of the transient quality of my feelings or thoughts.

There was great relief in this discovery for me, as I hope there will be for you! Those fleeting thoughts of lust, hate, and covetousness are not signals of impurity of heart. They are, like so many evidences of our humanity, a part of our present condition. Their presence does not exclude us from the promises to the pure in heart.

The inner quality that purity of heart does imply, however, is honesty with oneself, about oneself. C. S. Lewis in *The Screwtape Letters* has the chief devil, Screwtape, tell one of his subordinates, Wormwood, that if he is to be successful in misdirecting human beings, he should learn to exploit the human's unfortunate ability to lie to himself and believe the lie. Whether or not the devil makes us do it, the human tendency is to see oneself in a distorted fashion. Only when a person becomes willing to make a go at real self-knowledge is he in a position to display purity of heart in his relationships.

What, then, are the overt characteristics of those who are pure in heart? First and foremost, there is an absence of a manipulative quality in their relationships. They are not interested in changing or using their friends. To be a friend to these persons is to be accepted as you are and to feel confident that you will not be used as a means to a selfish end.

This unwillingness to use others is a very uncommon quality. Unfortunately, we are a part of a society that not only approves of manipulative relationships, but rewards the manipulator generously. The person who can sell another something he doesn't need, charm a group into supporting him and his cause, or "con" people within the boundaries of the law is highly sought after and very well paid. The positions of power are not often occupied by the pure in heart. They belong to the people who use people.

These little manipulations of others are so commonplace in our society that they generally go unnoticed and, if noticed, unchallenged. It's just the way things are—the way the up-and-at-'em people live.

Consider the case of the newcomer to a city who joins every organization he can—luncheon clubs, lodges, professional organizations, and the church—not so much because he wants to support the goals of these institutions, but because he hopes the members will come to know him, trust him, and do business with him. Think of how most of us have tried to impress our children with the need to be honest by advising them that "honesty is the best policy." The message is not that honesty is right and God demands it. It's that honesty, in the long run, will do more for you than dishonesty. We have even inserted a manipulative quality into our teaching of morality.

Maybe it would get even more sticky if we dared to face the manipulative quality often present in the professional world—particularly the white collar segment of it. I've already mentioned the much-maligned salesman. Let's get off his back for awhile and think of professors who get their hard work done by students who idolize them. Let's be objective about executives who buddy-buddy underlings into top production. We might even dare to turn a penetrating gaze at physicians, dentists, and lawyers whose bedside, chairside, and deskside manners bind people to them—people with whom, for the most part, they want very little to do socially.

Then, God help us, there are the clergy and the quasi-clergy. Guided by an end-justifies-the-means mentality, large numbers of those in church leadership positions have skillfully manipulated the faithful. With a seeming lack of confidence in the power of the gospel and the purposeful work of the Spirit of God, these ministers have harnessed the pulpit, the written word, and the electronic media to Madison Avenue manipulative techniques. In some instances, one is convinced that "there's no salesman like a God salesman."

Yet, while manipulation is commonplace in our society, let it be noted that the pure in heart are present, too. They still live as caring family members, as dedicated practitioners of the professions and as guileless proclaimers of the Word of the Lord. Even more pertinent is the fact that there is within most of us at various times both the person-using and the person-serving components. Indeed, our struggle for integrity in relationships is a very real part of our pilgrimage. The honest, growing Christian periodically must try to evaluate his relationships—his marriage, his parenting, his roles in the church, and his role at work—and weed out the person-using aspects of those relationships. Purity of heart does not come easily to most of us.

There seems to me to be one other component of purity of heart. It is a quality of openness. The open person lets you into himself. He is willing, at the proper time, to tell you who he is.

A friend of mine sent me a greeting card a few weeks ago. On the front it said: "Let's share our lives, our love and the deepest secrets of our souls." Upon opening the card, the instruction was, "And you go first!" The pure in heart are willing to go first. They are less interested in impressing you than they are in really meeting you in a deep encounter. In their openness— their sharing—there is a childlike trust.

This is not to be confused with a "get it all off your chest" kind of honesty. Some people have gathered the idea from popular psychology that they have the right, even the obligation, to tell you all their thoughts, deeds, and feelings— particularly as they relate to you. This may make them feel better, but it will probably make you (the recipient of all of this) feel worse. This is not the kind of openness characteristic of the pure in heart. The open, trusting, sharing person makes you feel better, not worse—stronger, not weaker. He is the interpersonal giver. She is the healer of battered persons.

I am intrigued by the idea that those special

moments in our lives in which we have felt drawn close to another may be described as meetings of the pure in heart. For a brief time in each encounter, whether between new or old friends, two people meet and share. There are no unspoken agendas. At that moment, neither wants to convince or change or use the other. It is a soul-to-soul meeting, and it is indescribably helpful and memorable.

I remember an encounter of this nature that I had a few months ago. For some reason, I attended a meeting of the county Psychological Association. Though I'm a dues-paying member, I seldom make the meetings. A few minutes into the social hour of this particular meeting, I remembered why I had quit attending. I was bored and tired of watching us try to impress each other. Perhaps it was his look of loneliness or my own feeling of being alone in a crowd, but I felt drawn to a studious-looking young man who was sitting by himself at a table.

The conversation began in a routine fashion. I talked of my work and listened as he told me of his position with a local university. Somewhere along the line, the conversation changed levels. He was a struggling Christian, too; so we talked of faith, of doubt, and of hope. They held the business meeting without the two of us that evening. While they met, we met. There was a trusting openness in our encounter that I have seldom experienced. That existential loneliness was gone and a sense of genuine oneness with another had taken its place.

Months have passed, and we have yet to meet

again, but we will. The next time it may be different, though I think we'll both remember for a long time—maybe even a lifetime—when we "accidentally" met soul to soul.

It is this kind of relationship which the healthy Christian is capable of in his best and healthiest moments, and it is this sort of encounter that is outside the experience of the emotionally ill.

"Healthy are the open, nonmanipulative persons."

EIGHT
*The
Peacemaking
Christian*

*"Happy are those
who work for peace
among men. . ."* ❧

In a world cursed by conflicts, this beatitude has a poignant ring. We need to find these makers of peace. We need to become one of them, for our world desperately needs them. But what are their attributes? Perhaps we can best arrive at a description of the peacemakers by eliminating some very destructive kinds of behaviors that often masquerade as peacemaking in nature.

In his book *Games People Play*, Eric Berne labeled one of his unhealthy interpersonal games as "Let's you and him fight." As a child, I used to play this one. The grade school I attended was really a tough one, populated for the most part by the children of steelworkers. Most of the boys in my grade seemed to feel that it had not been a good week if they had not witnessed a first-class fist fight in an alley near the school. I can report as both a spectator and combatant that these were fights of the blood-drawing and bruised face variety.

Some weeks, though, a good fight was hard to come by. No great issue arose on the playground that would result in a challenge to a post-schoolday fistic duel. On those weeks the fight had to be "worked up." The tactic was to send a note to a prospective pugilist (usually one of the really mean guys), stating that another fellow in the room had made a less than complimentary remark about him. The fires would be fanned a little during the rest of the day, and the probability was that we would have a good fight to attend at four o'clock.

I remember, now, as I reflect on it that I sometimes felt guilty about my part in the fight promotion. I remember, too, some bloody noses and bruised ribs that I experienced when I happened to have been one of the main-eventers. It all seems so childish now. To be grown-up is to have "put away childish things"!

Or is it? The truth is that I still see people playing this childish game. Call it "real friendship," "being honest," or gossiping—the results are usually deep hurt and damaged relationships. It is a kind of sickness that motivates a person to pass on hurtful information, even if it's true. To create a conflict for its entertainment value and for the enhancing of one's own sense of worth at the expense of others has never been a sign of health or of Christian discipleship. I can't tell you the amount of personal pain I have experienced because of information, the delivery of which was prefaced with, "There is something I simply must tell you," or "I feel that you need to know. . . ."

My pain is not to be compared, though, with the anguish I have known others to have experienced after the troublemakers told their stories. There was the woman who was told of her husband's infidelity by "a friend," three years after the fact. That little piece of information brought intense pain to both the wife and the repentant husband. The children knew their parents went through a bad period, but they never quite understood why the family moved to another town. I can only pray that the crisis this couple endured eventually resulted in a stronger, more satisfying relationship for them.

Then, there is the story of the young woman who could never quite escape her past—a past that contained the birth of an illegitimate child. She was too poor and lacking in job skills to move far from the scene of her mistakes. Supposedly well-meaning and God-fearing people seemed dedicated to sharing this information with everyone from employers to boyfriends. The last I heard from her, she was holding on to sanity by her fingernails—the victim of gossiping troublemakers.

These messages did not produce peace. They created turmoil. I even suspect that the bearers of the bad tidings found a kind of sick pleasure or sense of self-righteousness in another's pain. Though this is bizarre behavior, it is not unusual. The Christian landscape at times seems littered with broken persons, the victims of those who produce pain and conflict instead of peace.

Let's shift, now, from the sick to the sane. Peacemakers are not Pollyannas who refuse to recognize interpersonal differences and conflicts. There is no health in self-imposed ignorance. I have to confess that there is a trace (or more) of this behavior in me. I don't like conflict! When it comes, my reflex reaction is to look the other way and deny its existence. However, this denial does not produce peace. If the conflict is between another and me, looking the other way and refusing to deal with the issue allows me to engage in what I call "marks on the wall" behavior. "You did it to me—and that's one." Since the issue is not resolved and you may not know you have offended me, the probability is that you will repeat the offensive behavior. "You did it to me again, and that's two." The marks multiply—and by the time my anger forces me into conflict with you, the issue (and my resentment) is bigger than life. Behavior that began as an honest effort to avoid conflict ends up producing a conflict out of all proportion to the real or imagined affront. Also, I have denied you the opportunity to respond to my discomfort and change your behavior. Clearly, trying to deny conflict is not healthy, constructive behavior.

In the practice of marital therapy, I often observe this behavior and its results. Suddenly, or so it seems to the partner, a spouse announces his dissatisfaction with the marriage and, usually, his determination to "get out." He has counted up his "marks on the wall," and to his way of thinking there are enough to turn in for a divorce. This allergy to conflict and the ensuing compilation of unpleasant memories have led to the dissolution of a lot of once-happy relationships. All of this in the name of "keeping peace in the family"?

Some persons are inveterate troublemakers! The longer I work with people the more convinced I am that mentally unhealthy persons thrive on social turmoil. It seems that the person who is buffeted by the cross-currents of internal conflict does not feel at home in a tranquil environment. If the environment is disturbed, at least he does not feel like an alien. Often he will thrive. During wartime, for instance, there seems to be a lower incidence of incapacitating emotional illness. The internal problems are there, but the troubled person functions rather well in a troubled world.

So the sick person intuitively creates turmoil. He will transmit gossip or engage in painful and unnecessary confrontations. He will, in many devious ways, often unconsciously, fan the destructive fires of interpersonal conflict. It is almost an axiom for me—"Unhealthy are the troublemakers." If you're looking for the healthy ones among us, pass the troublemakers quickly.

Enough, though, of the negative. What does a genuine peacemaker look like? As I was searching through my past for memories of peacemakers, I was disturbed by the fact that the images of troublemakers emerged quickly to consciousness. It was more difficult to remember the peacemakers. I also found that, for the most part, I only call them peacemakers in retrospect. What they were about simply did not dawn on me in the moments—or years—of my closest association with them. Now, when I translate this concept into persons, pictures of some really special people come to my mind.

On my list of these special people is an uncle who good-naturedly bridged gaps in the family and refused to participate when his siblings chose up sides. There is Merri Lee, our youngest, who seems not to have time to create or participate in conflict. Life, for her, is too crowded with positive, beautiful activities and challenges. And then there is Betty. She was my secretary for nine years, and only now—some six years later—am I beginning to recognize the peacemaking qualities of her life. Betty could remind me of work to be done without seeming to nag. When I was angry with a parishioner, she calmed me, first with understanding, then with observations about the virtues of that person. She knew my faults and many of my secrets, but she kept them to herself. Bless you, Betty. I know now, better than before, that you are one of God's special peacemakers!

What, then, are the components of a healthy life style that distinguish these spreaders of good will? First of all, they have the ability to absorb information without feeling compelled to pass it on. President Truman made the slogan "The buck stops here" popular. The presence of that plaque in the Oval Office served as a reminder to him and all others who saw it that ultimate human responsibility for decision making was an integral part of the presidency. In similar fashion, healthy Christians provide a stopping place—a repository—for potentially hurtful information. Without trying to attribute qualities to them that make them sound like disposable diapers, let's say that they have a high absorptive quality. They have no great need to prove their worth by revealing what they know. They have enough ego strength not to have to make others look bad so they will look better.

Think of that person to whom you go when

you just have to "get something off your chest."
These are not your best moments, you know.
You reveal the darker side of your personality
and talk about your anger, resentment, guilt,
jealousy, and other all-too-human emotions.
Those meetings help, though, whether they are
with a professional or just a friend. You leave
that encounter with your tension reduced. You
feel better. You have "gotten it off your chest."
You have been with a peacemaker.

In the wake of a session like this, you may be
embarrassed at having put what you consider to
be your worst foot forward, but you seldom
worry about the security of your confidential
communication. You have trusted a
peacemaker—and your friend is strong enough
to be worthy of that trust.

There is almost an aura around the
peacemaker. One gets the feeling that as the
emotionally unstable person feels more
comfortable in the middle of turmoil and creates
it for his own comfort, so the peacemaker finds
tranquility to be his natural environment and
creates it. He is so at peace that his presence
promotes peace. Introduce this special type of
person into a disrupted group, and he will bring
calmness, rationality, and hope.

Peacemaking, though, must not be defined as
basically passive, and the peacemaker must not
be viewed as a passive person. He works! He
works for honest and peaceful relationships
between himself and others. He actively passes
on the Good News that can produce
intrapersonal peace. When those around him are

divided and hostile, he will become "a bridge over troubled waters." It is in the nature of bridges to get walked on, and so it is with the peacemakers. They give themselves to their friends and run the risk of rejection in their pursuit of peace between others.

But they cannot do otherwise. They have found peace, and it is in them to pass it on.

"Healthy are those who are at peace with themselves and others and who are passing on that peace."

NINE
The
Committed
Christian

*"Happy are those
who are persecuted
because they do
what God requires . . ."*

To the casual reader, this statement of the Teacher must sound like the motto for masochists. What healthy person would line up for reviling, persecution, and false accusations? To choose this would, indeed, be sick behavior.

Behavioral scientists spend a lot of time shaking their heads in near disbelief at the way some people jockey themselves into a position to suffer psychic stress and pain. They are bewildered, too, by others who set themselves up for physical pain, like the woman I knew some years ago who averaged almost an operation a year. Her belly must have looked like a patchwork quilt, and one can only wonder why physicians joined in her "operation of the year" game. She had a definable mental illness.

Then there are those persons who need to fail. Just when things seem to be going well, count on them to foul up. They are convinced, at some psychic level, that they do not deserve success—that they are unworthy of feeling good. They muddle through a lifetime, if they are not helped, constantly torpedoing themselves. Obviously, this is not healthy behavior!

There are, of course, those persons mentioned earlier for whom pain translates into pleasure. They are wired up wrong. Only to feel good when one feels pain is an emotional illness. We call it masochism.

These sufferers are in trouble. My friend with the surgically scarred belly was not well. The scuttler of his own success is sick. The masochist, we all agree, has a deep-seated emotional problem. Jesus, in this beatitude, is not trying to make the sick look well. He is not extolling deviant behavior!

What, then, is the point? How does this statement about suffering fit into my thesis about the life style of the mentally healthy person? The key is that Jesus was not talking about suffering as an indicator of health. He was talking about the reason for suffering and malignment as a component of healthy living.

Why the suffering described in this last beatitude? It was for "his sake." The straightforward message about these healthy persons was that they had found and embraced a cause. For them, there was something in life greater than themselves. They had found a Person, an idea, for which they would suffer, and if necessary, die.

The themes of emptiness, meaninglessness, and futility have been strong in literature from the earliest times. Read Solomon's story in the book of Ecclesiastes. If you fail to read the last chapter, the book is a dismal indictment of life and all its achievements. Life is "vanity and vexation of spirit," and there is very little meaning "under the sun." Try the writings of the secular existentialists, like Sartre and Camus, and you end up with a haunting sense of human futility. American novelists like Fitzgerald and Hemingway pick up on the theme. Life is a disappointment. At the end there is only a big, fat zero.

Check out our experience with the young in our society. The sixties produced a cause—the cause of peace—and our youth latched onto it.

Some went to Viet Nam, and others went to the streets. A few went to Canada. So great and emotional was the response that one got the feeling that this is what the youth of the sixties were looking for—a cause. When it was all over, some of these kids returned to their routines—sad, somewhat disillusioned and empty. They would tell you that they missed—almost longed for—the unrest, the challenge that called out decision and commitment in them.

The seventies have witnessed the return to the traditional by our children. They are back in the classroom, not to disrupt but to learn. They seldom get into the streets. They are intent on pursuing the goal of professional and economic achievement. Like their fathers, they have yet to learn that "a man's life does not consist in the abundance of the things that he possesses." They are great candidates either now or later for the classic middle class American illness—depression. They really have no consuming commitment, except, perhaps, to the dollar. Life does not seem as zesty for them as for their brothers and sisters in the turbulent sixties. And the suicide rate for adolescents and young adults has climbed to an alarming level.

The trouble is that there is in the soul of every person a need for commitment to a great big cause. Without some all-consuming purpose for which to live and die, a person is not alive at the highest level. Until one finds that cause, he is the center of the universe. The largest of all issues are his health and happiness. When the cause is found and a commitment is made to it, the person has moved outside himself. He is still important, but not all-important. He still seeks happiness, but not at all costs.

In a way, this is what the Austrian psychiatrist, Victor Frankl, identifies as the foundation of mental health—a sense of meaning for one's life. According to Frankl, a person loses zest and desire for life if he does not have an identified purpose for his existence.

To illustrate his point, Frankl tells of his concentration camp experience during World War II. He spent several agonizing years as an incarcerated Jew. Being a scientist, he tried to observe and draw knowledge from his fellow prisoners. He took note of the fact that some died very quickly after being pushed through the gates, while others who were not physically stronger than their fellows seemed to refuse to die.

He searched for that quality that separated the ones who seemed to choose to live from those who gave up and died. Soon he discovered the difference. Those who lived had a reason to live. Those who died very quickly had no reason left for living.

Every person is in search of something greater than himself to which he can dedicate his life and death. And Christ provides that cause. He demands love, obedience, and hard work. Healthy is the person who "takes up his cross daily" and follows him. He has found his cause.

For the people who embrace the Jesus-cause, there is also a sense of eternity. The healthy person is not unduly frightened by the certainty of his own death. There are a lot of people in our world who are so afraid of death that they can't enjoy life. Like the coward, they "die a thousand deaths." The person Jesus describes in this beatitude knows that suffering and death are not ultimates for him. Joy and life are the ultimates. He had committed himself to an eternal, not a temporal cause.

As a very young minister, I had a classic lesson in the kind of health that helps a person live and die. The lesson was given me by a special friend who was an aging druggist in the little town where I was pastor of the Baptist church. He had time between filling prescriptions, and I had time between my pastoral chores; so we passed many an hour talking over a marble-topped table in his drugstore. We conversed about everyday things—but we also talked a lot about dreams and goals. He had wanted to be a physician, but he had not had money enough for a medical education. Pharmacy was close to medicine—and it was the best he could do; so he became a pharmacist.

We talked about more than dreams. We often talked about faith. His faith was tough and real. It had been questioned and tested dozens of times. Mine was still a bit soft, a little on the inherited side. Those talks helped me. He was tough-minded and still trusted in God. This combination provided an ideal for me to try to emulate.

Then there came the day that the doctors told

my friend he was terminally ill with cancer—a fast-growing and painful type of the dreaded disease. Now we really communicated. He declined rapidly, but he always was willing to report to me on his state of mind and state of health. He had depressive episodes. He questioned the rightness of it all. He told me of his apprehensive dread of dying. But he still trusted in God.

I guess I wondered if his faith would endure the ultimate test of his dying. I hoped it would, but feared it would not. Somehow I was "going to school" on his experience.

My friend sent for me when he was dying. I ran the block and a half from my office in the church to the little hospital where he had spent his last few weeks. I paused outside the door to his room and prayed I would be able to stand the experience that was just beyond that door. I had never before stood close to the dying process.

When I entered the room, my friend's wife leaned over and said into his ear, "Don is here," and he motioned me to his side. He was gasping for breath and speaking with difficulty. He tried to say something to me; so I leaned close and listened. He was saying, "Pray, Don." I thought, "This is it, and he is afraid. His faith cannot stand the ultimate test." Finally, I choked back my tears and asked a question. "For what do you want me to pray, Brother Crane?" Then came the answer. "Thank him, Don. Thank God for the Cross." I said the prayer, and I thanked God for the Cross and the empty tomb. Soon my friend met the Father to whom he was grateful. Faith and hope and eternity filled that room in the wake of his dying. Those moments had given meaning to his life and had authenticated his faith—and mine.

Paul wrote about this healthy faith when he said, "I am convinced that the sufferings of the present life are not to be compared with the glory that shall be revealed in us." This is our hope, and in this hope there is health. Death is not the end. It is an event in our everlasting lives. Suffering is real—but it is not the ultimate reality. Beyond all of this there is God—and good and joy and life.

So it is not suffering itself that is a sign of health. It is the fact that the person has found a cause for which he is willing to suffer that is a sign of health. Death, of course, is not a sign of health. We all will die. It is the fact that eternity is present in a person's dying that signals health.

Mark it down. The healthy person finds meaning in life—and in death.

"Healthy are those who have a cause for which to live and who find in it purpose, even for dying."

TEN
Gifts for the Healthy

We have, now, in these eight terse statements of Jesus, a verbal portrait of a healthy Christian. We also have come face to face with the difficulty of the divine assignment. How in the world are we to put all of this into practice all of the time? It's possible to feel a little sick and quite spiritually destitute when one compares his own life style with the portrait of the healthy Christian that the Teacher drew for us. In spite of our study, efforts, and prayers, we are a long way from where we ought to be. These statements prove that!

It is precisely this feeling of personal spiritual inadequacy that should send us back to reread the first (and keystone) beatitude, "Healthy are those who know they are spiritually poor." Jesus must have started with that principle because he knew that an honest application of the other seven might drive us to despair. We are spiritually poor, and there are elements of sickness in the personality of each of us. And that's OK.

It's OK because we have become aware of two concepts—directionality and grace. Directionality tells us that we can live without having arrived at a state of perfect health if we are moving in the right direction. It's being on the road toward health that helps us live with our imperfection. The illness in us—that distance between where we are on the road toward health and where we ought to be—is blanketed by God's grace. He forgives us our trespasses and our illness while we are on that journey.

The sensitive pilgrim finds an old-time prayer echoing in his soul:

Oh, Lord, I'm not what I should be,
I'm not what I want to be,
I'm not what I'm going to be,
But, thank you, Lord, I'm not what I used to be.

In poetic fashion, each of the descriptive statements about the healthy Christian is balanced with a promise. It is obvious that, to this point, I have not dealt with those promises. It's not that they are unimportant. It's just that they are not of *primary* importance to the healthy Christian. The person described in the first half of the beatitude is not that kind of person because he wants to reap the rewards of good behavior. He is a healthy person because of his nature and his careful learning of a Christian life style. He welcomes the promises and their fulfillment, but he has found at a very deep level that health is its own reward. Being mentally healthy feels good. It makes him capable of experiencing genuine joy. His relationships are strong and supportive. He doesn't have to be enticed toward health by a big carrot in the sky.

". . . THE KINGDOM OF HEAVEN
BELONGS TO THEM."

I like the promises Jesus makes to the honest, though perhaps unspectacular, disciples. Isn't it encouraging to know that the kingdom of heaven does not belong to self-anointed super saints who leap over church steeples in single bounds? Rather, the kingdom of heaven is in the care of those who know they are spiritually poor and those who have discovered in the risen Jesus a person and a cause for which they can live and die.

If William Barclay is correct when he asserts that this kingdom is present at that point in time and space at which a Christian does the Father's will, then it is easy to see why the kingdom belongs to these to whom it was promised. It is present when a believer struggles toward his goals. It is evident in every deed that is done "for Jesus' sake." These struggling and dedicated persons are the tenants and workers of the kingdom—and their lives and activities are evidence of its reality.

Indeed, the kingdom of heaven does belong to these special people, and it seems to me that it is in capable hands.

". . . GOD WILL COMFORT THEM."

It's beautiful that God has promised to be actively involved in comforting his mourning children. Having tasted the griefs and limitations of humanity, our Lord knows the pain. What more human description could be given of the Christ than the one used by the prophet Isaiah—"a man of sorrows and acquainted with grief"? Isn't there great meaning in the statement in Hebrews that affirms his oneness with us by saying, "He was tempted in all points as we . . ."? He *does* know the need we all have for divine help. He knows that to be human is to

117

experience grief because he's walked this human road.

The comforting of his children was so paramount in the plan of God that Jesus gave a special name to the spiritual presence of God in each of us. He named that presence the Comforter. That Comforter is here to help us deal with life's great crises—and even with its little annoyances. All of us have observed Jesus keeping his promise of comfort. We have watched the healing of a person crushed by grief and have listened as the person thanked God for the comfort of his unfailing presence. Others of us have been there and know from our own anguished experience that God does, indeed, comfort his mourning children.

". . . THEY WILL RECEIVE WHAT
GOD HAS PROMISED."

Isn't it special, too, that teachable people stand ready to receive God's promises fulfilled in their lives? This promise suggests that the closed-minded may be shutting out a lot of the excitement and beauty that the Father intended for them to experience. It's the child-like, open, curious, and impressionable Christian who comes closest to experiencing the full measure of God's promises. It takes openness to be a recipient of a gift. Many have found in their own experience that to receive a gift takes more love than to give one. It's easier to hear than to say a sincere "thank you."

Those, however, who are open to God—those who trust his purposes for them—hold up open hands, not clenched fists, to the Father. And when the gifts come, they receive them with gratitude and without doubt as to the source.

". . . GOD WILL SATISFY THEM FULLY."

In a generation characterized by restlessness, emptiness, and an endless desire for change, the idea of a completely satisfied person is hard to comprehend. Such, though, is the promise of the Teacher to those who passionately desire to do the Father's will. Living among us are those healthy people who, in doing the will of God, have found peace and satisfaction. They are not constantly driven to be different. They really want nothing more than they have. God has satisfied them fully, as he promised.

What further proof of the good intentions of God for each of us do we need? In doing his will we reach our full human potential. There is no sense of incompleteness or waste. This healthy person has found and is doing the will of God—and, in contemporary jargon, it is his thing.

". . . GOD WILL BE MERCIFUL TO THEM."

To the merciful, Jesus promises mercy. What better gift could he give them? These people are well acquainted with the high incidence of sin and injustice in the world and are painfully aware that they have been the victims of some of it. After all, to be forgiving one must first be wronged. Undoubtedly these sensitive people also know their own need of mercy. They have learned, too, through their own experience, that mercy is not cheap. It always costs the giver.

The cost of mercy to God is all wrapped up in the Calvary scene. "By his stripes we are healed." To be extended mercy by our fellow humans is to receive a great gift—but the forgiveness of *God* is the most costly gift of all. The magnificence of the gift of mercy cannot be lost to the merciful.

". . . THEY WILL SEE GOD."

Like Moses on the mountain, it seems that man has always had a deep desire to see his Heavenly Father. God has tried to accommodate us within our mortal capabilities. He allowed Moses a glimpse—but not of his face. He came in flesh to the earth to show us the qualities of the Divine in a form we could come close to understanding. The quest, however, for the real face of God continues. How beautiful it is that to the pure in heart the promise comes—"They shall see God."

What does this promise really mean? Is the Teacher saying that some of our contemporaries will have an experience denied to Moses on Mount Sinai? Or is he saying, as most seem to believe, that someday in heaven these people will see God? In my judgment, Jesus is saying neither of the above. Instead, the promise is that these beautiful, guileless people will be able to see God in places and in persons while others of us will miss Him. They will be confronted by the Father in his creation, and they will stand stunned at the sense of his presence. They will see God in people and be awed that God has for a moment shown them himself. The scales of cynicism are removed from the eyes of these